TALK YOUR BOOK

SAY IT, SHAPE IT, SHARE IT

JORI O'NEALE

Copyright © 2025 by Jori O'Neale
All rights reserved.

No part of this publication may be reproduced, distributed, or transmitted in any form or by any means, including photocopying, recording, or other electronic or mechanical methods, without the prior written permission of the publisher, except in the case of brief quotations embodied in critical reviews and certain other noncommercial uses permitted by copyright law.

Published by
The 1 and Only Publishing
4500 Forbes Blvd
Lanham, MD 20706
www.the1andonlypublishing.com

ISBN (Paperback): 979-8-89741-028-6
ISBN (eBook): 979-8-89741-029-3

Printed in the United States of America

Cover design and interior formatting by **The 1 and Only Publishing**

For more information on publishing your own book, visit www.the1andonlypublishing.com

To My Family
May you always know the role you play in helping me to carve out time to talk all the books God put on my heart to pen.

CONTENTS

Introduction: You Don't Need to Write to Be a Writer 1
Chapter 1: Believe Before You Write 5
Chapter 2: Time + Habits for Voice-First Creators 13
Chapter 3: Prompted on Purpose 23
Chapter 4: Speak in Color, Not Chaos 33
Chapter 5: From Voice Notes to Structure 41
Chapter 6: Story Frameworks That Work 51
Chapter 7: Transcribe and Transform 61
Chapter 8: Publish Without Permission 69
Chapter 9: Build Your Audience Before You Launch 81
Chapter 10: Monetize the Message 91
Conclusion: Say It Again 101

INTRODUCTION

You Don't Need to Write to Be a Writer

SOME OF US were never meant to write books the "normal" way.

The blinking cursor. The stiff outlines. The pressure to sound smart. The rules about what a "real writer" is supposed to do? They never worked for me—and maybe they haven't worked for you either.

Listen, I've been there. Sitting at my computer, staring at that mocking cursor, feeling like I had to sound like some fancy author instead of just being me. Trying to follow all the writing rules when my brain doesn't work in straight lines. Believing I needed perfect grammar before I could share my story, when really, I just needed to get it *out*.

Here's what I discovered after 22 years of storytelling, after helping hundreds of women birth their books, after realizing that some of the most powerful stories I've ever heard came tumbling out of women's mouths during our sessions, not from behind computer screens:

You don't need to write to be a writer.

I built this book for the neurodivergent dreamers, the time-poor creatives, the multi-passionate folks who are ready to birth something bold... even if they don't think they're writers.

If you think better out loud, if you tell stories with your whole body, if your best ideas come mid-conversation—you're my people. If you've been told you talk too much, share too openly, or get too animated when you're passionate about something—honey, those aren't bugs, they're features.

The seed for this book was actually planted during a conversation with Michele DeFilippo, founder of 1106 Design, who has helped over 4,000 authors publish like pros. During our podcast interview, she said something that made my whole spirit leap: "People's stories want to breathe. Their book wants to get out and you help people do that."

And my response? "Get it out. Let's go. Let's go. Let's get it out."

That's what this book is about. Getting it out. Not perfectly. Not according to someone else's timeline or rules. But authentically, powerfully, in a way that honors how your brain actually works.

This book will walk you through a voice-first process—one built around prompts, story snapshots, and emotional clarity. You'll move from audio to outline, and eventually from voice notes to a published book that sounds exactly like you, because it *is* you.

We're going to work with your natural rhythms instead of against them. We're going to honor the fact that your voice—the one that shows up when you're explaining something you're passionate about to a friend—is already perfect for your book.

Let's talk your book.

CHAPTER 1

Believe Before You Write

*"You didn't just help me write a book.
You helped me believe again."*
— Christina

THE BIGGEST LIE we've been told about writing is that you have to be a "writer" to write a book.

But here's what I know after watching woman after woman transform from "I'm not a writer" to published author: you don't need to identify as a writer. You just need to believe your story matters.

And if you picked up this book, some part of you already knows it does.

THE FALSE BELIEFS THAT KEEP US STUCK

Let me tell you about Christina. When we first met, she'd been trying to write her book for *years*. She had the story—a powerful journey about finding authentic beauty and identity beyond corporate success. She had the passion. She had the calling.

What she didn't have was permission to sound like herself.

"I keep trying to sound like someone else," she told me during one of our sessions. "Like I need to be more professional, more polished. But then it doesn't sound like me anymore."

Sound familiar?

Here are the false beliefs I hear most often—and why they're keeping you stuck:

"Real writers suffer through the process." Who decided that writing had to be torture? Yes, birthing anything meaningful requires effort, but it doesn't have to feel like you're dragging yourself through broken glass. When Christina discovered she could speak her book instead of typing it, she said, "Wait, I can just talk? And that becomes my book?" The relief in her voice was everything.

"I need to sound like other authors." Christina kept trying to write like the business books she'd read, losing all her personality in the process. When she finally stopped performing and started speaking authentically about her journey from corporate burnout to purpose-driven life, magic happened. Her voice—warm, honest, real—came through every word.

"I don't have time to write a book." This one breaks my heart because it's usually said by women who are already telling their stories every day. Christina was working full-time, managing a business, dealing with health issues, and still found time to birth her book by speaking it during her commute and lunch breaks.

"If I can't write like [insert famous author], I shouldn't write at all." Roz worried about this constantly. "What if it's not good enough?" she'd ask. But here's the thing: the world doesn't need another version of someone else's voice. It needs the first version of yours.

HOW SPEAKING UNLOCKS YOUR TRUTH

Let me share what happened during Christina's breakthrough session.

She'd been stuck on her book about burnout and misalignment for months. Every time she sat down to write, she'd get tangled up in trying to sound "professional" or "authoritative." The words felt stilted, disconnected from the raw truth of what she'd experienced.

So I asked her to stop writing and just talk to me like she was explaining to a friend what burnout really felt like.

What poured out was stunning:

"It's a complete depletion. If you can imagine... your whole body is weak and your mind is foggy and nothing makes sense. When I ended up in the hospital for five days, my body was reacting to an ovarian cyst that burst, but my mental state was telling my body to go in the hospital. Like it was literally shutting down."

That wasn't clinical. That wasn't detached. That was *real*. That was the voice her readers needed to hear—someone who had walked through the fire and could guide them through it too.

When you speak your story instead of writing it, you bypass all the internal editors and critics. You access the part of your brain that knows how to connect with people, the part that naturally builds tension and releases it, the part that understands timing and emphasis.

Speaking out loud helps you uncover your truth because:

Your voice has natural rhythm. When Christina spoke about her burnout, she automatically paced her story for maximum impact. She paused when she talked about being in the hospital. She emphasized the words that mattered.

You include the human details. Her spoken story included texture—how her body felt, what it was like to be misunderstood, the specific moment she realized something had to change.

You connect with emotion, not just facts. She wasn't just reporting what happened. She was sharing what it felt like to live through it.

You speak to a real person, not an imaginary audience. Even though we were in a coaching session, Christina was naturally speaking to the women who would need her story—women feeling trapped in corporate burnout, wondering if there was another way.

Permission to Start Messy

Christina said something during one of our sessions that I'll never forget: "I feel like I understand the assignment now."

What was the assignment? To stop trying to be perfect and start being real.

Here's what I need you to understand before we go any further: Your first draft is supposed to be terrible.

I know, I know. Everyone talks about "crappy first drafts," but nobody really believes it applies to them. You think your story needs to emerge fully formed, like Athena springing from Zeus's head.

But here's the truth: Every good book starts as a mess. Every single one.

When I showed Christina how to use voice-to-text on

Google Docs, her whole face lit up. "Wait, so I can just push this button and talk, and it shows up on the page?"

Exactly.

We even recorded her saying punctuation marks out loud—"comma," "period," "new paragraph"—so her transcripts would be cleaner. She thought it was weird at first, but then she realized: this was working *with* her brain instead of against it.

The difference between people who finish books and people who don't isn't talent or education or natural writing ability. It's the willingness to be bad at something long enough to get good at it.

And speaking your story gives you permission to be messy in the most productive way possible.

Building Trust with Yourself

The work of writing a book isn't really about learning to write. It's about learning to trust yourself.

Trust that your story matters. Trust that your voice is enough. Trust that you don't need permission from anyone else to claim your space as an author.

Roz struggled with this trust. She kept asking, "But what if people don't want to read it? What if it's not professional enough?"

During our call, I could hear the wisdom in her voice, the years of experience, the heart for helping others. "Roz," I said, "you just talked for twenty minutes about why this book matters, and I was hanging on every word. *That's* your book voice."

That trust builds one conversation at a time, one voice note at a time, one "what if I just said it like I'd say it to my sister" at a time.

Christina learned this when she realized her story wasn't just about corporate burnout—it was about the lie that success could be her savior. "Success is not your savior," she said during one session, and I stopped her right there. "That's your book title."

Sometimes the most important thing you'll write is hiding in plain sight, waiting for you to say it out loud.

The Courage to Begin

What noise do you need to close the door on?

Maybe it's the voice that says you need an MFA to write a book. Maybe it's the relative who told you that you "talk too much." Maybe it's the writing teacher who red-penned your essays until you stopped trying to sound like yourself.

Whatever it is, it's time to close that door.

Because on the other side of that closed door is your voice. And your voice—exactly as it is, with all its imperfections and personality and passion—is what the world is waiting to hear.

Christina said it best: "You didn't just help me write a book. You helped me believe again."

That's what this process does. It helps you believe again—in your story, in your voice, in your right to take up space on the bookshelf.

Voice Prompts for Chapter 1

Before you move to the next chapter, I want you to practice what we just talked about. Get out your phone, open your voice recorder app, and answer these prompts out loud. Don't think too hard. Just talk.

Prompt 1: What false beliefs have I had about being

a writer? *Speak for 2-3 minutes about the stories you've told yourself about who gets to write books and why you might not qualify.*

Prompt 2: How has speaking out loud helped me uncover my truth in other areas of my life? *Think about times when talking through a problem helped you figure it out, or when you surprised yourself with what came out of your mouth during an important conversation.*

Prompt 3: What do people always come to me for advice about? *Often, the thing you naturally help others with is exactly what your book should address.*

Remember: There are no wrong answers here. The goal isn't to sound polished or profound. The goal is to get comfortable with the sound of your own voice telling your truth.

After you record your responses, listen back to them. Notice how you naturally emphasize certain words. Pay attention to the places where emotion comes through in your voice. Hear how you explain things in a way that makes sense, using your own words and your own rhythm.

That's your writing voice. Not the voice you think you're supposed to have, but the one you already do have.

Trust it. It knows exactly what it's doing.

CHAPTER 2

Time + Habits for Voice-First Creators

"Having someone cheer me on gave me the permission I didn't know I needed to start."
– Corina

THE SECOND BIGGEST LIE we've been told about writing (after "you have to be a writer to write a book") is that you need big blocks of uninterrupted time to make meaningful progress.

But here's what actually happened when Corina finally finished her book:

She spoke it into existence during her morning coffee ritual, fifteen minutes at a time, before her household woke up. She captured story fragments during her lunch breaks at work. She recorded voice memos while walking her dog, processing the emotions that needed to make it onto the page.

No writing retreat. No sabbatical. No perfect home office with the ideal lighting and noise-canceling headphones.

Just fifteen minutes here, twenty minutes there, and the radical belief that small, consistent actions could birth something beautiful.

WHEN YOUR BRAIN WORKS DIFFERENTLY

Let me tell you about the conversation that changed everything for how I think about time and creativity.

During our podcast interview, I asked Michele DeFilippo—who's helped over 4,000 authors publish—about the biggest obstacles authors face. Her response wasn't what I expected.

"The workflow," she said. "People don't generally know what the workflow is. They think they can just sit down and write a book, but there's quality control at every step."

But here's what she missed—and what traditional publishing has missed for decades: not everyone's workflow looks the same.

Some of us are neurodivergent. Some of us are raising small humans. Some of us work three jobs. Some of us think in spirals instead of straight lines. Some of us have brains that light up during conversations but shut down in front of blank pages.

The writing industry has been built around a very specific type of person: someone who can sit still for long periods, who thinks linearly, who has the luxury of uninterrupted time.

But what if you're not that person?

What if your brain needs movement to think? What if you process ideas better out loud? What if your most creative moments happen while you're doing dishes or driving carpool?

That doesn't make you less of a writer. It makes you a different kind of writer. And different kinds of writers need different kinds of systems.

DESIGNING RITUALS THAT WORK WITH YOUR NEUROTYPE

Corina discovered this accidentally. She'd been trying to write her book the "normal" way for years—sitting at her computer during whatever time she could carve out, usually late at night when she was already exhausted.

"I kept waiting for the perfect time," she told me. "Like, when the kids are older, when work slows down, when I have more energy. But that time never came."

Sound familiar?

Then something shifted. Instead of waiting for the perfect time, she started using the time she actually had.

"I realized I was already talking about my book ideas," she said. "When I was explaining to my sister why I wanted to write it, when I was processing my thoughts with my therapist, when I was answering questions from friends who'd heard I was writing. I was already creating the book—I just wasn't capturing it."

So she started capturing it.

Her phone became her writing tool. The voice memo app became her manuscript. Her morning coffee ritual became her writing time—not because she had hours to spare, but because she had fifteen minutes and finally understood that fifteen minutes was enough.

Here's what she learned about designing sustainable creative habits:

Start with your natural rhythms. Corina is a morning person who thinks best before the world makes demands on her attention. So she claimed those fifteen minutes before anyone else was awake. If you're a night owl, claim the evening. If you think best while moving, record while you walk.

Work with interruption, not against it. Traditional writing advice tells you to find uninterrupted time. But what if interruption is part of your reality? Corina learned to work in fragments—one story per voice memo, one chapter per week, one emotion at a time. The interruptions actually helped her process.

Use encouragement as fuel. "Having someone cheer me on gave me the permission I didn't know I needed to start." Corina didn't just need a system; she needed support. She started sharing voice memos with a trusted friend who would text back with encouragement. That accountability became part of her creative ritual.

Honor your processing style. Some people need to think before they speak. Others need to speak to think. Corina discovered she was definitely the latter. "I didn't know what I thought about my story until I heard myself telling it," she said.

THE MYTH OF "FINDING" TIME

Here's what nobody tells you about time: you don't find it. You create it.

Every successful author I've worked with has had to get creative about when and how they write. Not because they're special or disciplined, but because they stopped waiting for ideal conditions and started working with real ones.

Christina recorded her burnout story during her commute. Voice-to-text while stuck in traffic became her manuscript.

Roz found her voice during evening walks, processing the stories she wanted to tell the women she mentored about resilience and faith.

Eugenia discovered that the painful memories from her medical journey could only be accessed when she was doing something with her hands—cooking, folding laundry, moving her body while her mind traveled back through her experiences.

None of them had extra time. They all had the same 24 hours we all have. What they had was permission to work differently.

THE POWER OF MICRO-SESSIONS

Let me share some math with you that might blow your mind.

- Fifteen minutes a day, five days a week, for twelve weeks equals fifteen hours of voice recording.
- Fifteen hours of speaking can easily become 40,000-50,000 words when transcribed.

40,000-50,000 words is a book.

Which means you can write a book in the time it takes most people to scroll through social media each day.

But here's the key: those fifteen minutes have to be consistent, and they have to be intentional.

Not fifteen minutes of "trying to think of what to say." Not fifteen minutes of staring at your phone wondering if you sound stupid. Fifteen minutes of answering specific prompts that help you excavate the stories that are already inside you.

Christina figured this out when she stopped trying to

write chronologically and started responding to questions:

"What moment made you realize you needed to change your life?" "What would you tell your younger self about the struggle you went through?" "What lie did you believe that kept you stuck?"

Each question became a voice memo. Each voice memo became a chapter. Each chapter became part of her story.

ENERGY MANAGEMENT OVER TIME MANAGEMENT

But here's what's even more important than time management: energy management.

You can have all the time in the world, but if you're trying to write when your brain is fried, you're not going to create anything worth reading.

But you can't create your best work when you're running on empty.

This is why the voice-first method works so well for busy people. Speaking requires less cognitive energy than writing. When you're tired, you can still tell a story. You might not be able to craft beautiful sentences, but you can share what happened and how it felt.

The crafting comes later. The capturing happens when you have the energy for it.

Corina learned to track her energy alongside her time. She noticed she was most emotionally available for the heavy parts of her story in the mornings. Her voice was clearest then, her defenses were down, her willingness to be vulnerable was highest.

So she used morning time for the deep stuff and saved easier topics—practical advice, lighter stories, conclusions—for evenings when she was winding down.

"I stopped fighting my natural rhythms," she said. "I started designing my book around how I actually live."

CREATING YOUR SUSTAINABLE SYSTEM

Your writing habit doesn't have to look like anyone else's. It just has to work for you, consistently, over time.

Here's how to design a system that honors your real life:

Audit your current time. For one week, notice when you naturally find yourself telling stories, processing thoughts out loud, or explaining things to people. These moments are already happening—you just need to start capturing them.

Identify your peak energy times. When do you feel most emotionally available? Most creative? Most willing to be vulnerable? Those are your prime writing times, even if they're only fifteen minutes long.

Choose your capture method. Voice memos on your phone. Voice-to-text in Google Docs. A simple audio recorder. The tool doesn't matter as much as your comfort with using it.

Design your prompts. Have specific questions ready so you don't waste time wondering what to talk about. We'll dive deep into this in the next chapter.

Build in support. Whether it's a writing buddy, a coach, or just someone who checks in on your progress, don't try to do this alone. Even if you're an introvert, even if you prefer working independently, some form of encouragement and accountability will help you finish.

Plan for imperfection. You're going to miss days. You're going to record things you hate. You're going to feel like you're not making progress. Plan for this. It's part of the process, not a sign that you should quit.

Corina missed an entire week when her kid got sick. Instead of giving up, she used naptime to record one voice memo about how hard it is to pursue dreams while handling real life. That voice memo became one of the most powerful chapters in her book.

PERMISSION TO START WHERE YOU ARE

The enemy of finishing your book isn't lack of time. It's the belief that you need different time—more time, better time, uninterrupted time—than what you actually have.

But your book doesn't need ideal conditions. It needs your voice, captured consistently, over time.

It needs you to stop waiting for someday and start with today.

It needs you to believe that fifteen minutes of honest storytelling is infinitely more valuable than three hours of staring at a blank page.

Corina's book exists because she finally gave herself permission to start where she was, with what she had, for as long as she could manage.

Your book is waiting for the same permission.

VOICE PROMPTS FOR CHAPTER 2

Set a timer for 15 minutes and record your responses to these prompts. Don't overthink it—just press record and start talking.

Prompt 1: When do I feel most creative or clear? Think about the times of day, activities, or environments when your best ideas come to you. Be specific. Is it during your morning shower? While you're cooking dinner? During your commute?

Prompt 2: What has kept me from starting or continuing my book before? Be honest about the real obstacles—not the ones you think you should have, but the ones you actually face. Is it perfectionism? Fear? Overwhelm? Lack of clarity about your message?

Prompt 3: What would my ideal creative routine look like if I designed it around my real life instead of my fantasy life? Forget the writer's retreat or the perfect home office. If you had to create a sustainable writing practice within your current reality, what would it look like?

After you record these, listen back and notice patterns. Your voice already knows what you need—you just have to get brave enough to honor what it's telling you.

CHAPTER 3

Prompted on Purpose

"I had all these ideas. You gave me the roadmap."
— Laurie

THE THIRD LIE we've been told about writing is that inspiration just strikes, and when it does, you better be ready with your laptop and your perfect environment and your uninterrupted time.

But here's what I've learned after helping hundreds of women birth their books: inspiration isn't some mystical force that descends from the heavens. It's a skill you can develop, a muscle you can strengthen, a GPS system you can learn to operate.

The secret isn't waiting for the right feeling. It's asking the right questions.

THE MESSAGE THAT'S WAITING INSIDE

During my conversation with Michele DeFilippo, she said something that stopped me in my tracks:

"Any book can be fixed. This is what the specialists in the industry do."

But then I realized: you can't fix what doesn't exist. And most people never get to the fixing stage because they're stuck at the starting stage, staring at the blank page, waiting for the words to come.

Michele talked about market research, about looking for burning problems that lots of people have. "If you have the answer to that problem," she said, "then you can write a book that has a better chance to sell than if you just get a bright idea."

That's smart business advice. But it misses something crucial: sometimes the problem you're meant to solve is hiding inside your own story, waiting for the right question to excavate it.

Take Michele herself. During our interview, she talked about how she got into publishing "entirely by accident." She never planned to become the woman who would help over 4,000 authors publish their books. She just responded to opportunities as they came, pivoted when technology changed, kept solving problems for authors who needed help.

But buried in that "accidental" story was deep wisdom about resilience, about building a business around service, about staying mission-focused for over 50 years. She just needed the right questions to help her see the book that was already living inside her experience.

WHAT PEOPLE ALWAYS COME TO YOU FOR

Here's a question that unlocks more books than any other:

"What do people always come to you for?"

Not what you think you should be an expert on. Not what your degree is in or what your job title says. What do people actually seek you out for when they need help?

Sometimes it's obvious. Terry Williams knew people came to him about building coaching frameworks because he'd developed his own successful system and other coaches were asking how he did it.

But sometimes it's subtle. Roz didn't think of herself as having expertise until I asked her this question. Then she realized: people had been coming to her for decades for advice about faith, about perseverance, about how to keep believing when life gets hard.

"I never thought of that as expertise," she said. "That's just... life."

Exactly. That's just life. Your life. The life you've lived, the lessons you've learned, the wisdom you've earned through experience.

The most powerful books aren't written by people with fancy credentials. They're written by people who've been somewhere their readers need to go.

THE FIVE-YEAR-AGO TEST

Here's another question that consistently unlocks book ideas:

"What do I wish I had a book for five years ago?"

This question does something magical: it takes you back to a time when you were in the thick of whatever struggle or transition you've since navigated. It helps you remember not just what you learned, but what you desperately needed to hear.

When I asked Tracy this question during our workshop, her whole face changed.

"Five years ago, I was still trying to figure out my spiritual identity, feeling disconnected from my higher purpose. I was searching for meaning but didn't understand how to get back to who I was really meant to be. I wish I'd had a book about spiritual transformation, about finding your way back to your authentic self."

There it was. Her book. Not a theological treatise (though it includes deep spiritual insights). Not a memoir about her specific journey (though it's deeply personal). A book for the woman she used to be, written by the woman she'd become.

Sia answered this question differently: "Five years ago, I was still carrying shame about my story. I thought my experiences were too heavy, too specific to my culture, too painful to share. I wish I'd had a book that showed me how healing could come through storytelling, how my specific story could speak to universal human experience."

USING PROMPTS AS GPS

Here's what most people don't understand about prompts: they're not meant to give you answers. They're meant to help you discover what you already know.

Your story is already inside you. Your wisdom is already earned. Your message is already formed. You just need the right questions to help you excavate it.

Think of prompts like a GPS system for your inner landscape. You wouldn't try to navigate to a new city without directions. But somehow we expect people to navigate their way to a book without any guidance about where to look for their stories.

The prompts I use with clients aren't random. They're designed to help you:

Access emotion, not just events. "What happened" is facts. "How it felt" is story. The prompt "What's a memory that plays in your mind like a movie?" gets to the felt experience, not just the chronological facts.

Identify transformation, not just experience. Anyone can list things that happened to them. But a book needs to show change, growth, learning. "What lie did you believe that kept you stuck?" helps you identify the before-and-after that makes your story worth sharing.

Connect personal to universal. Your specific story matters because it illuminates something universal. "What do you wish someone had told you?" helps bridge the gap between your experience and your reader's need.

Find your unique angle. "What do people misunderstand about [your experience]?" helps you identify what you have to say that hasn't been said before.

THE HEALING POWER OF THE RIGHT QUESTIONS

But here's something that surprised me when I started using this voice-first method: the prompts don't just help you discover your book. They help you heal your story.

Michele talked about this during our interview, though she might not have realized it. When I asked her about her 50+ years in publishing, she started seeing patterns she'd never noticed before. How she'd been problem-solving for authors her entire career. How every pivot and transition had been in service of helping people get their stories out into the world.

"I really should probably just start saying it would take a year if you're only at the idea stage," she mused, "because I'm sure they delay you sometimes as they delay us."

But then she caught herself. "You know what? My granddaughter has issues in that area. Yeah. But there's a will, there's a way, right? I think sometimes God wants us to have the difficulty so that we become better."

See how the conversation moved from business advice to personal revelation? That's what the right questions do. They help you see your own wisdom, your own growth, your own healing journey.

PROMPTS FOR DIFFERENT PARTS OF YOUR JOURNEY

Not all prompts work for all parts of your story. Just like you wouldn't use the same GPS coordinates to navigate to your house and to a new restaurant, you need different questions to access different aspects of your experience.

For accessing the beginning of your story:
- "What moment made you realize things needed to change?"
- "What lie were you believing about yourself/life/success?"
- "What question did you start asking that changed everything?"

For processing the middle—the struggle, the journey:
- "What was the hardest part that no one talks about?"
- "What kept you going when you wanted to quit?"
- "What did you have to let go of to move forward?"

For identifying transformation and wisdom:
- "What do you know now that you wish you'd known then?"
- "How are you different because of what you went through?"
- "What would you tell someone who's where you used to be?"

For connecting to your reader:
- "What do people get wrong about [your experience]?"
- "What do you wish more people understood about [your topic]?"
- "What question do you get asked most often?"

WHEN YOU THINK YOU DON'T HAVE A STORY

Sometimes people tell me, "I don't have a dramatic story. Nothing terrible happened to me. Who am I to write a book?"

But here's what I've learned: the most powerful books often come from ordinary people who've found extraordinary wisdom in everyday experiences.

Roz worried about this. "My story isn't as dramatic as some people's," she said. "I haven't overcome addiction or survived trauma or built a million-dollar business."

But when I asked her, "What do people always come to you for?" she lit up.

"Faith," she said immediately. "People ask me how I stay so positive, how I keep believing when things get hard. They ask me how I raised kids who still love Jesus, how I've stayed married for 40 years, how I find joy in small things."

That's not a small story. That's a story about how to live

well, how to find meaning in ordinary moments, how to be a person others turn to for hope.

The prompt that unlocked her book was simple: "What wisdom have you learned through just living life that you think other people need to hear?"

YOUR STORY GPS

The beautiful thing about using prompts is that they meet you wherever you are in your story and help you find your way forward.

If you're stuck in the pain and can't see the purpose yet, prompts help you access the feelings without having to have all the answers.

If you're past the struggle but not sure how to make it helpful to others, prompts help you bridge the gap between your experience and your reader's need.

If you know what you want to say but don't know how to organize it, prompts help you find the natural structure that's already there.

Michele said something during our interview that I keep thinking about: "You've got to get that into your subtitle or your marketing message or something that you're coming at it from the theater perspective. Because that separates you from everybody who claims to be a ghostwriter."

She was talking about how my theater background makes my approach different. But the deeper truth is this: everyone has something that makes their approach different. Everyone has a unique angle, a particular wisdom, a specific way of seeing the world.

You just need the right questions to help you discover what it is.

PERMISSION TO EXPLORE

Here's what I want you to understand before we start excavating your story: you don't have to know where the prompts will lead you.

The point isn't to have a complete book plan before you start speaking. The point is to start speaking and see what emerges.

Some of your responses will surprise you. Some will feel obvious. Some will make you cry, and some will make you laugh at yourself.

All of that is information. All of that is your story finding its way out.

Trust the process. Trust your voice. Trust that the right questions will unlock exactly what needs to be unlocked, when it needs to be unlocked.

Your book is already inside you. We're just going to ask it some questions and see what it has to say.

VOICE PROMPTS FOR CHAPTER 3

Remember: there are no wrong answers. The goal is discovery, not perfection. Set your timer for 20 minutes total and respond to these prompts out loud.

- **Prompt 1: What do people always come to me for?** (5 minutes) Think broadly—advice, perspective, help with specific problems, a listening ear. What do friends, family, coworkers, even strangers consistently seek you out for?
- **Prompt 2: What do I wish I'd had a book for five years ago?** (7 minutes) Go back to where you were five

years ago. What were you struggling with? What questions were you asking? What kind of guidance were you desperately seeking? Be specific about what you needed to hear.

- **Prompt 3: What wisdom have I learned through just living life that I think other people need to hear?** (8 minutes) This isn't about dramatic transformation or overcoming huge obstacles. This is about the insights that have come to you through experience—about relationships, work, faith, parenting, creativity, resilience, joy. What do you know now that you didn't know at 25?

After you record these responses, listen back with curiosity rather than judgment. What themes emerge? What surprises you? Where do you hear passion in your voice?

Those passion points? That's where your book lives.

CHAPTER 4

Speak in Color, Not Chaos

*"Talking helped me process what I didn't
even know I was holding onto."*
— Sia

THERE'S A MOMENT in every storytelling session when something shifts.

The person stops reciting facts and starts painting pictures. Their voice changes—becomes more animated, more present, more alive. They stop telling me what happened and start showing me how it felt.

This is when the real book begins.

It's the difference between reading a police report and watching a movie. Between hearing about someone's experience and feeling like you lived it yourself. Between information and transformation.

Your voice already knows how to do this. You just need permission to let it.

THE THEATER IN YOUR VOICE

Every book I write, I want it to be a movie. I need to see the struggle, feel the transformation, experience the journey right alongside the character.

This isn't because I'm being dramatic (though my theater background definitely influences how I think about story). It's because the human brain is wired for visual, emotional storytelling. We remember feelings, not facts. We connect with scenes, not summaries.

When Sia first started talking about her book during our workshop, she began with the facts: where she was born, when she came to America, the basic timeline of her experiences.

It was accurate. It was informative. But it wasn't alive yet.

But then something shifted when she started describing the emotional landscape of her story. Her voice changed—became more present, more powerful.

"This is a transformative book, and it's so emotionally painful," she said. "As I write it, there's a healing process going through. This is a universal story. It's not just a story that came from Africa, but it's a human story."

Now we had the real book. Not just events, but transformation. Not just what happened, but what it meant.

"Talking helped me process what I didn't even know I was holding onto," Sia told me later.

FINDING THE MOVIE MOMENTS

Your story is full of movie moments. Times when you can remember not just what happened, but how the light looked, what you were wearing, what you could smell, what you were thinking.

These moments are your story's superpowers. They're the scenes that will make your readers lean in, hold their breath, see themselves in your experience.

But most people skip over them. They think they need to stick to the "important" parts—the decisions, the turning points, the lessons learned. They give me the executive summary when what their book needs is the director's cut.

Here's what I've learned about finding those cinematic moments:

- **They're often small.** Not the moment you quit your job, but the moment you sat in your car in the parking lot afterward, hands shaking as you called your mom. Not the day you got married, but the morning of, when you looked in the mirror and realized you were becoming someone's wife.
- **They include sensory details.** The coffee that tasted like cardboard during your worst day at work. The way your daughter's hair smelled when she hugged you after you finally left your toxic relationship. The sound of your own voice saying "I can't do this anymore" for the first time.
- **They reveal internal experience.** What were you thinking? What were you afraid of? What were you hoping? The external events are just the stage—the real story is what was happening inside you.

- **They show contradiction.** The moment you felt powerful and terrified at the same time. When you were grateful and angry. When you knew you were doing the right thing but it felt like everything was falling apart.

COLORS AND FEELINGS VS. FACTS AND TIMELINES

During my workshop with Tracy, we talked about the emotional landscape of transformation. But here's what struck me: you need to create emotional honesty in your storytelling, not just chronological accuracy.

Not just what happened, but how it felt. Not just the outcome, but the texture of the experience.

When I ask someone, "What color or feeling describes your story?" they usually laugh at first. "What do you mean, color?"

But then they get it.

"It's gray," Tracy said about her period of spiritual searching. "Everything felt muted, like I was seeing life through a fog. But then there were these moments of gold—when I'd catch a glimpse of who I was supposed to be."

These aren't abstract concepts. These are the emotional landscapes of their stories. And when they speak from these feelings instead of from facts, their voices become magnetic.

THE VULNERABILITY ADVANTAGE

Sia talked about something during our workshop that I think about often: how telling your story requires both courage and boundaries.

"It's extremely healing," she said about her writing process. "But it's things that I have to put down and step away from sometimes."

You have to be willing to go to the real places, the messy places, the places where you weren't the hero of your own story. But you also have to know how much to share and when.

Speaking your story out loud helps you calibrate this. Your voice will naturally find the right level of vulnerability–deep enough to be real, boundaried enough to feel safe.

When you're typing, it's easy to either sanitize your story (making it so clean it loses all its power) or overshare (giving readers more than they need or you're comfortable with). But when you're speaking, you naturally modulate. You share what feels right to share in the moment.

LAYERING TONE AND MOOD

Your voice carries information that typed words can't convey. Pace. Emphasis. Emotion. Subtext.

When you slow down on certain words, you're telling your future readers: this matters. Pay attention here.

When your voice gets quiet, you're creating intimacy.

When it gets stronger, you're building momentum.

When you pause, you're giving space for the weight of what you just said to land.

All of this gets lost when you start with typing. But when you start with voice, it's all there in the recording. Your transcriptionist or editor can see it. You can feel it when you listen back.

This is part of protecting your creative process: honoring the natural rhythm and tone of your voice instead of trying to force it into someone else's cadence.

METAPHOR AS YOUR SECRET WEAPON

Here's something that happens almost every time: when people speak their stories, metaphors emerge naturally.

"It felt like I was drowning in my own life."

"I was carrying this invisible weight everywhere I went."

"It was like I'd been speaking a foreign language for years and finally found someone who understood my native tongue."

These aren't forced literary devices. They're how your brain naturally makes sense of abstract experience by comparing it to concrete images.

When you're typing, you might edit these out, thinking they're too casual or not sophisticated enough. But these organic metaphors are often the most powerful parts of your story. They help readers connect their experience to yours. They make the invisible visible.

Don't edit them out. Lean into them. Let your voice find the comparisons that make your experience make sense.

THE EMBODIED STORY

When people speak their stories out loud, their whole body gets involved. Hands move when they describe key moments. Shoulders shift when they talk about carrying emotional weight. Voices break in exactly the right places.

This is embodied storytelling—when your whole self is engaged in the telling, not just your mind.

You can't fake this. You can't manufacture it by sitting at a computer and trying to remember how you felt. But when you speak your story out loud, your body remembers. Your voice carries the emotional memory.

This is why voice-first storytelling creates such authentic, compelling narratives. Because they're not just coming from your head. They're coming from your entire lived experience.

PERMISSION TO BE CINEMATIC

Here's what I want you to understand: your story is already cinematic. Your life is already full of scenes worth watching, moments worth remembering, transformations worth witnessing.

You don't need to add drama. You just need to pay attention to the drama that's already there.

You don't need to make your story more interesting. You need to tell it in a way that reveals how interesting it already is.

Your voice knows how to do this. It's been doing it every time you've told someone about something that really mattered to you. Every time you've made someone laugh or cry or lean in closer because they had to hear what happened next.

That's the voice your book needs. Not the voice you think you should have, but the voice you already do have when you're sharing something that matters.

VOICE PROMPTS FOR CHAPTER 4

Get comfortable and press record. Let yourself speak with the same energy you'd use if you were telling these stories to your best friend.

- **Prompt 1: What's a memory that plays in your mind like a movie?** (7 minutes) Choose a moment from your

journey that you can see clearly in your mind. Don't just tell me what happened—paint the scene. Where were you? What did you see, hear, smell? What were you wearing? What was the weather like? What were you thinking? Take me there with you.
- **Prompt 2: What color or feeling describes your story?** (5 minutes) If your whole journey had a color palette, what would it be? If it had a texture—smooth, rough, jagged, soft—what would that be? If it had a temperature, a weather pattern, a landscape? Don't overthink this. What images come to mind?
- **Prompt 3: What metaphor naturally describes your experience?** (8 minutes) How would you explain what you went through to someone who's never experienced anything like it? What would you compare it to? A storm? A journey? A death and rebirth? A puzzle? Let your mind make connections and see what emerges.

Listen back to these recordings and notice how your voice changes when you're painting pictures versus when you're just sharing information. That shift—that's where your book lives.

CHAPTER 5

From Voice Notes to Structure

*"My message was there all along—
I just needed a map."*
— Terry

THE DIFFERENCE BETWEEN a powerful story and a confusing ramble isn't the quality of the material. It's the structure that holds it all together.

But here's what most people get wrong about structure: they think they need to figure it out before they start speaking. They think they need an outline, a plan, a complete roadmap before they record their first voice note.

That's backward.

Your structure is already there, hiding inside your voice notes. You just need to learn how to find it.

THE MESSAGE THAT WAS ALWAYS THERE

Terry Williams came to me with boxes of content. Literally boxes. Years of coaching notes, workshop materials, client testimonials, half-finished chapters. He had enough material for three books, but he couldn't see the book for the trees.

"I know there's something here," he told me during our first session. "I've been helping people for years. I have frameworks that work. But every time I try to organize it all, I get overwhelmed."

Sound familiar?

Terry had fallen into the trap that catches most subject-matter experts: he was trying to include everything instead of focusing on the one thing that mattered most.

So I asked him a simple question: "If you could only teach someone one thing—the thing that would make the biggest difference in their life—what would it be?"

Without hesitation, he said: "That they already have everything they need to succeed. They just need a system to organize it and the confidence to trust it."

There it was. His book. Not a comprehensive guide to everything he'd ever learned about coaching. Not a memoir about his journey from struggling entrepreneur to successful mentor. A book about helping people recognize their existing resources and organize them for maximum impact.

"My message was there all along," he said later. "I just needed a map."

THE NATURAL STRUCTURE IN YOUR VOICE

When you speak your story out loud, your voice naturally creates structure. You emphasize certain points. You pause for effect. You circle back to important themes. You build to climaxes and give space for resolution.

All of this is structural information. Your voice is already organizing your material—you just need to learn how to see it.

Here's what I listen for when I'm helping someone find their book's structure:

- **What do they keep coming back to?** The themes that show up repeatedly across different voice notes are usually your main points. If you mention "learning to trust myself" in three different recordings about three different situations, that's probably a chapter.
- **Where does their energy change?** When someone's voice gets more animated, they're hitting something important. When it gets quieter and more intimate, they're sharing something vulnerable that readers need to hear. These energy shifts mark the emotional beats of your book.
- **What questions do they naturally answer?** Often, people will pose questions as they're speaking: "You might be wondering why I stayed so long..." or "The real question isn't whether you're ready..." These questions reveal the structure your reader's mind is following.
- **How do they naturally sequence events?** Some people tell stories chronologically. Others jump around in time but follow an emotional logic. Others organize around lessons learned. Your natural sequencing style is probably the right structure for your book.

TERRY'S FRAMEWORK: THE 4 CS AND 4 FS

During our work together, Terry developed what he called his organizing principle—a way to think about transformation that helped both him and his clients see the structure in their growth.

The 4 Cs represented the internal work:

- Clarity (getting clear on what you really want)
- Courage (facing the fears that keep you stuck)
- Consistency (showing up even when you don't feel like it)
- Community (finding the people who support your growth)

The 4 Fs represented the external actions:

- Focus (narrowing down to what matters most)
- Framework (creating systems that support your goals)
- Feedback (learning from what's working and what isn't)
- Forward movement (taking action even when the path isn't clear)

This wasn't something he sat down and invented. This was the pattern that emerged when we looked at all his client success stories and asked: "What do people who achieve transformation consistently do differently?"

The framework was already there in his work. We just had to extract it from all the other material and organize it in a way that made sense.

FROM AUDIO TO OUTLINE: A STEP-BY-STEP PROCESS

Here's the process I use with clients to turn voice notes into book structure:

Step 1: Record without editing. Don't worry about organization. Just answer prompts and tell stories. Get the raw material out of your head and into audio files.

Step 2: Listen for themes. After you have 5-10 voice recordings, listen through them and note what keeps coming up. What words do you use repeatedly? What concepts do you return to? What questions do you naturally address?

Step 3: Group similar content. Take your themes and start clustering your voice notes around them. All the recordings about overcoming fear go in one pile. All the ones about practical strategies go in another. All the ones about mindset shifts go in a third.

Step 4: Find your natural sequence. Look at your clusters and ask: If someone was learning this for the first time, what order would make the most sense? What do they need to understand first before they can grasp the next concept?

Step 5: Identify the gaps. Once you can see your natural outline, you'll notice what's missing. Maybe you have great content about the problem and the solution, but nothing about the journey in between. Maybe you have powerful stories but no practical application. Those gaps become prompts for additional voice notes.

Step 6: Test your structure. Tell someone your book idea using your new structure. Can they follow it? Does it make sense? Where do they get confused? Their questions will help you refine your organization.

SCENES VS. SUMMARIES

One of the biggest mistakes people make when organizing their book is thinking in summaries instead of scenes.

A summary is: "I learned to trust my intuition."

A scene is: "I'm standing in my boss's office, and he's offering me the promotion I've wanted for three years. But something in my gut is screaming 'no.' For the first time in my life, I listen to that voice instead of the voice that says I should be grateful for any opportunity."

Scenes are what make books memorable. Summaries are what make them forgettable.

When you're structuring your voice notes, look for the scenes—the specific moments when something shifted, when you learned something important, when you had to make a difficult choice.

These scenes become the backbone of your chapters. The lessons and insights that emerged from those moments become the meat around the bones.

THE ONE-MESSAGE TEST

Here's how you know you've found your book's true structure: you can explain the entire book in one clear message.

Not one sentence—that's your hook. But one coherent message that connects all your points and tells someone exactly what they'll get from reading your book.

Terry's message became: "You already have everything you need to create the life you want. This book will help you recognize your resources, organize them effectively, and take action with confidence."

Every chapter in his book supports that message. Every

story illustrates it. Every practical exercise helps readers implement it.

If you can't explain your book's message clearly, your structure isn't quite right yet. Keep working with your voice notes until the through-line becomes obvious.

STORY FRAMEWORKS THAT ACTUALLY WORK

Different types of books need different structural approaches. Here are the ones I use most often with voice-first authors:

The Journey Framework (for transformation stories):
- Where you started
- What made change necessary
- The process of transformation
- Where you are now
- How others can make their own journey

The Problem-Solution Framework (for how-to books):
- The problem everyone faces
- Why previous solutions don't work
- Your approach
- How to implement it
- What success looks like

The Teaching Framework (for expertise-based books):
- What you've learned
- How you learned it
- Why it matters
- How to apply it
- What's possible when you do

The Story Collection Framework (for books built around multiple experiences):
- The theme that connects all stories
- Story 1 + lesson
- Story 2 + lesson
- Story 3 + lesson
- How all lessons work together

The framework you choose should feel natural to how you already talk about your topic. If you're a storyteller, use the journey or story collection framework. If you're a teacher, use the teaching or problem-solution framework.

Your voice notes will tell you which one fits.

WHEN STRUCTURE SERVES STORY

Good structure is invisible. Readers shouldn't notice your organizational system—they should just feel carried along by the logic of your message.

That's why I always tell clients: structure serves story, not the other way around. If your organizational system is making your content feel forced or artificial, the structure needs to change, not the content.

Terry discovered this when he tried to force his material into a traditional business book format. It felt rigid and lifeless. But when we organized it around his natural teaching style—the way he actually worked with clients—everything clicked.

"I was trying to write the book I thought I should write instead of the book I actually wanted to write," he said.

Your voice notes contain the book you actually want to write. Trust them. Let them show you the structure that serves your message instead of forcing your message into someone else's structure.

THE MAP YOU'VE BEEN LOOKING FOR

Remember: your book's structure isn't something you impose on your material. It's something you discover within it.

Your voice already knows how to organize information in a way that makes sense. It already knows how to build tension and resolve it, how to sequence ideas logically, how to help people follow your thinking.

You just need to listen to what it's telling you.

Terry's material was never disorganized. It was just waiting for the right map to reveal the order that was already there.

The same is true for your voice notes. The structure is there. The message is clear. You just need to learn how to see it.

VOICE PROMPTS FOR CHAPTER 5

These prompts will help you start identifying the natural structure in your story.

Prompt 1: What's one message I feel called to say in this book? (8 minutes) Not your hook or your elevator pitch, but the core message. If someone read your book and understood only one thing, what would you want that to be? How would their life be different because they received this message?

Prompt 2: If I told my story in scenes, what moments come first? (10 minutes) Think cinematically. What are the key scenes—the specific moments—that show your transformation or illustrate your message? Don't worry about order yet. Just identify the scenes that matter most.

Prompt 3: What pattern do I see in my own growth that might help others? (7 minutes) Looking back at your journey, what steps did you consistently take? What obstacles did you repeatedly face? What insights kept showing up? This is where your natural framework lives.

After recording these, listen for the themes that connect your responses. That connecting tissue is your book's structure starting to emerge.

CHAPTER 6

Story Frameworks That Work

*"I realized my life had chapters—
I just hadn't named them yet."*
— Terry

ONCE YOU HAVE your voice notes and you can see the themes emerging, the next question becomes: how do you organize this into something that feels like a real book?

This is where most people get stuck. They have powerful content, meaningful stories, important insights. But they can't figure out how to put it all together in a way that makes sense to a reader who doesn't live inside their head.

The answer isn't to follow someone else's rigid formula. It's to discover the framework that's already hiding inside your natural way of thinking and talking about your topic.

THE WRITE NOW ROADMAP

After working with hundreds of storytellers, I've developed what I call the WRITE NOW Roadmap–a flexible framework that honors how people actually process and share their stories, not how they think they're supposed to write books.

W–Whisper (the voice notes and raw capture) **R**–Retell (sharing and refining through conversation) **I**–Itemize (organizing themes and key points) **T**–Transcribe (turning audio into text) **E**–Edit (polishing and strengthening)

N–Navigate (understanding your reader's journey) **O**–Organize (creating your book's structure) **W**–Write (filling in gaps and connecting pieces)

Notice that traditional "writing" doesn't happen until step 7. That's intentional. By the time you get to actual writing, most of your book already exists in your voice notes. You're not creating from scratch–you're organizing and connecting what you've already captured.

WHO IS YOUR READER?

Before you can choose the right framework for your book, you need to get crystal clear about who you're writing for.

Not everyone. Not "people who might be interested." One specific person who represents your ideal reader.

Terry discovered this when we talked about his coaching business. "My reader is the person who has all the pieces but can't see how they fit together," he said. "They're capable, they're motivated, but they're overwhelmed by their own potential."

That clarity changed everything about how he organized his book. Instead of trying to cover every aspect of personal development, he focused specifically on helping people recognize and organize the resources they already had.

Tracy's reader became clear during our workshop: "Someone who feels spiritually lost, like they've drifted away from who they're supposed to be. They want to get back to their authentic self but don't know how to start."

Sia described her reader as "anyone who has been through trauma and thinks their story is too heavy, too specific, too painful to matter to anyone else. I want to show them that our specific stories speak to universal human experience."

THE JOURNEY VS. THE TEACHING

Most books fall into one of two categories: journey books or teaching books.

Journey books follow a transformation. They take readers from where they were to where they are now, showing the path of change. These work well for people who have overcome something significant or who have experienced a major life transition.

Teaching books organize around lessons or principles. They help readers understand concepts and apply them. These work well for people who have developed expertise or frameworks that help others succeed.

Some books are hybrids, but most lean heavily toward one approach or the other.

Terry's book was clearly a teaching book. He had frameworks, systems, and proven methodologies. His readers wanted practical tools they could implement.

Tracy's book was more of a journey book. Her readers needed to see the path from spiritual confusion to spiritual clarity, with practical steps along the way.

Sia's book was a journey book that would include universal lessons—showing her personal transformation while illuminating truths that apply to anyone healing from trauma.

FRAMEWORKS FOR JOURNEY BOOKS

If your book follows a transformation journey, here are the most effective organizational approaches:

The Before/During/After Framework:
- Where you started (the problem, the pain, the old way of being)
- The journey of change (what happened, what you learned, how you grew)
- Where you are now (the transformation, the new understanding, the different life)

The Catalyst Framework:
- The moment everything changed
- What you discovered about yourself/life/the world
- How you applied that discovery
- What became possible as a result

The Quest Framework:
- What you were searching for
- The obstacles you encountered
- The guides and tools that helped you
- What you found (and what you learned about the search itself)

FRAMEWORKS FOR TEACHING BOOKS

If your book shares expertise or methodology, these structures work well:

The Problem-Solution Framework:
- The challenge everyone faces
- Why traditional approaches don't work
- Your method/philosophy/approach
- How to implement it
- What success looks like

The Levels Framework:
- Foundation principles
- Intermediate applications
- Advanced strategies
- Integration and mastery

The System Framework:
- Component 1 + how to apply it
- Component 2 + how to apply it
- Component 3 + how to apply it
- How all components work together

Terry used a version of the System Framework, organizing his book around his 4 Cs and 4 Fs methodology. Each component became a chapter, with real client examples and practical exercises.

YOUR STORY'S NATURAL STRUCTURE

The most important thing to understand about frameworks is this: the right one for your book is the one that matches how you naturally think and talk about your topic.

During our workshop, I asked Tracy to tell me her book's core message in one sentence. She said: "They tasted independence when he offered intimacy."

That sentence revealed her book's natural structure. It's about the choice between self-reliance and divine relationship, about the journey from spiritual independence back to intimate connection with God. Her book naturally wanted to be organized around that tension and resolution.

When I asked Terry the same question, he said: "You already have everything you need to succeed—you just need to recognize it, organize it, and trust it."

That sentence contained his entire book structure: recognition (helping people see their existing resources), organization (providing systems to arrange those resources effectively), and trust (building confidence to act on what they know).

THE READER'S JOURNEY VS. YOUR JOURNEY

Here's a crucial distinction: your book's structure should follow your reader's journey, not necessarily your personal chronology.

What I mean is this: the order in which you learned things isn't always the best order for teaching them. The sequence of your life events isn't always the most compelling way to tell your story.

Your job is to organize your material in the way that best serves your reader's understanding and transformation.

Sometimes that means starting with the end—the insight or transformation—and then showing how you got there. Sometimes it means jumping around in time to group similar lessons together. Sometimes it means sharing your personal story as illustrations of larger principles rather than as a chronological narrative.

Roz understood this instinctively when we talked about her book. She didn't want to write a memoir that started with her childhood and went through her entire life. She wanted to organize around themes—faith, resilience, joy, community—and use stories from different periods of her life to illustrate each theme.

TESTING YOUR STRUCTURE

Once you think you've found your book's natural framework, test it. Tell someone your book idea using that structure. Can they follow it? Does it make sense? Where do they get confused or lose interest?

Their feedback will help you refine your organization.

Also test it with your voice notes. Do your existing recordings fit naturally into your proposed structure? Or are you trying to force your content into a framework that doesn't really match how you think?

If the structure feels forced, trust your instincts. Go back to your voice notes and listen for the natural organization that's already there.

THE FRAMEWORK IS NOT THE BOOK

Remember: choosing a framework is not the same as writing your book. The framework is just the skeleton. Your voice notes, stories, insights, and personality are the muscle, organs, and life force that make the skeleton into something readers will want to spend time with.

Don't get so caught up in finding the perfect structure that you forget to let your authentic voice come through. The best framework in the world won't save a book that doesn't sound like a real person talking about something they genuinely care about.

And don't be afraid to adjust your framework as you work. Sometimes you'll discover that your book wants to be organized differently than you initially thought. That's not a sign that you're doing something wrong—it's a sign that you're listening to what your book needs.

Terry told me: "I realized my life had chapters—I just hadn't named them yet." Your book has a structure too. You just need to discover what it is and give it the framework it deserves.

VOICE PROMPTS FOR CHAPTER 6

These prompts will help you identify your book's natural framework.

Prompt 1: Who is my reader and what struggle are they facing? (8 minutes) Be specific. Not "people who want to improve their lives" but "women in their 40s who feel like they've lost themselves in taking care of everyone else." What does their day look like? What keeps them up at night? What do they desperately want but don't know how to get?

Prompt 2: What part of my personal journey matches their pain? (7 minutes) Where in your story do you connect with their struggle? When were you where they are now? This connection point often reveals whether your book is more of a journey book or a teaching book.

Prompt 3: If I had to organize my book into 3-5 main sections, what would they be? (10 minutes) Don't overthink this. Based on everything you've recorded so far, what are the main chunks your book wants to divide into? Trust your instincts about what feels like natural groupings.

After recording these, you should have a clearer sense of your book's basic structure and whether it's primarily a journey book, a teaching book, or a hybrid of both.

CHAPTER 7

Transcribe and Transform

"I had the story, but you helped me make it a book."
– Roz

THERE'S A MOMENT in every voice-first book project when the magic happens.

You've been speaking into your phone for weeks, capturing stories and insights and wisdom. You have hours of audio files, dozens of voice memos, a collection of conversations that feel important but scattered.

And then you see it all transcribed for the first time.

Suddenly, what felt like random thoughts becomes a manuscript. What sounded like casual conversation reveals itself as chapters. What seemed like you just talking becomes a book that sounds exactly like you—because it is you.

But getting from voice notes to finished book requires more than just transcription. It requires transformation.

FROM AUDIO TO TEXT: THE TECHNICAL SIDE

Let's start with the practical stuff. You have voice recordings, and you need them turned into text you can work with. You have several options:

Automated transcription (like Otter.ai, Rev.com, or even Google Docs voice typing): Fast and inexpensive, but requires cleanup. Good for getting a rough draft quickly.

Professional transcription services: More accurate, especially with proper punctuation and speaker identification. Costs more but saves editing time.

Hybrid approach: Use automated transcription for speed, then have a professional clean it up. Good balance of cost and quality.

DIY transcription: You type while listening to your recordings. Time-consuming but gives you complete control over the process.

The method you choose depends on your budget, timeline, and how much editing you're comfortable doing. But here's what matters most: don't let the transcription process stop you from moving forward.

Perfect transcription isn't the goal. Getting your voice captured in text form so you can start working with it—that's the goal.

WHAT HAPPENS WHEN YOU SEE YOUR VOICE ON PAPER

Roz experienced something that happens to almost everyone who tries the voice-first method for the first time. She was worried about how her book would sound, whether it would be "professional enough," whether people would take it seriously.

Then she saw her transcribed voice notes.

"I had the story," she told me, "but you helped me make it a book."

What she realized was that her voice—the one she was worried wasn't good enough—was actually exactly what her book needed. It was warm, wise, accessible. It sounded like someone you'd want to sit with over coffee and learn from.

That's what happens when you see your authentic voice transcribed. You realize it's not rough or unprofessional—it's human. And human is exactly what readers are looking for.

THE ART OF VOICE-TO-TEXT EDITING

Transcribing voice notes isn't just about converting audio to text. It's about preserving the essence of your spoken voice while making it work on the page.

Here's what that process looks like:

- **Preserve your natural rhythm.** Your voice has a natural cadence, a way of emphasizing certain words and pausing at others. Good editing maintains that rhythm instead of flattening it into formal written prose.
- **Keep your authentic language.** The way you naturally explain things, the words you choose, the phrases you repeat—these are features, not bugs. Don't edit them out in favor of "better" vocabulary.
- **Add structure without losing spontaneity.** Spoken stories often loop back, circle around, build in layers. Some of this needs to be organized for readers, but not so much that you lose the organic flow of your thinking.
- **Clean up without sterilizing.** Yes, remove the "ums" and false starts. But keep the conversational tone, the personal asides, the moments where your personality shines through.

FILLING THE GAPS

Once you have your transcriptions, you'll start to see the shape of your book. You'll also see what's missing.

Maybe you have a powerful opening story and a clear conclusion, but the middle feels thin. Maybe you have great practical advice but no personal examples to illustrate it. Maybe you have emotional stories but no actionable takeaways.

This is normal. This is expected. This is why we don't try to create a perfect book in one recording session.

The gaps you identify become prompts for additional voice notes:

- "I need a story that shows what it looks like when someone applies this principle."
- "I need to explain how readers can start implementing this in their own lives."
- "I need to bridge the gap between this concept and that one."

Record these additional pieces the same way you recorded everything else—by speaking naturally into your phone, answering specific prompts that address what your book needs.

WORKING WITH PROFESSIONAL EDITORS

At some point, you'll want professional help polishing your manuscript. But working with an editor when you've used a voice-first approach is different than working with one when you've written traditionally.

Here's what to communicate to any editor you work with:

This started as spoken content. Help them understand that preserving your voice is more important than conforming to formal written standards.

Conversational tone is intentional. You're not trying to sound academic or overly polished. You want to sound like you're having a conversation with a friend.

Repetition might be purposeful. When you're speaking, you naturally emphasize important points by returning to them. Some of this repetition serves the reader and shouldn't be edited out.

Keep the personality. Your quirks, your humor, your way of explaining things—these make your book uniquely yours.

The right editor will understand this and help you create a book that sounds professionally polished while still sounding authentically you.

THE TECHNOLOGY THAT HELPS

The voice-first approach is easier now than it's ever been, thanks to technology that keeps improving:

Voice-to-text apps are getting more accurate at capturing natural speech patterns and even some punctuation.

AI editing tools can help clean up transcriptions while preserving conversational tone.

Cloud storage means you can record voice notes on your phone and access them from your computer for editing.

Collaborative platforms let you work with editors and other team members without losing track of versions.

But remember: the technology is just a tool. The real magic happens when you give yourself permission to speak your truth and trust that your voice is exactly what your book needs.

WHEN FEAR SHOWS UP IN THE EDITING PROCESS

Here's what happens to almost everyone when they see their transcribed voice notes for the first time: they panic.

"This doesn't sound like a real book." "This is too casual." "People will think I don't know what I'm talking about." "I need to make this sound more professional."

These fears are normal. They're also usually wrong.

What you're seeing isn't unprofessional writing—it's authentic communication. What feels too casual to you feels accessible and genuine to your readers.

The goal isn't to sound like every other book in your genre. The goal is to sound like you, but polished. Like the best version of how you naturally communicate.

Roz worried about this throughout our process. She kept asking whether her book would be "professional enough" for people to take seriously. But when she finally held her finished book—one that sounded exactly like her voice—she realized that "professional" doesn't mean "impersonal." It means "effective at helping people."

And her voice was definitely effective at helping people.

THE TRANSFORMATION ISN'T JUST IN THE TEXT

The most surprising thing about the voice-first approach isn't how it changes your book—it's how it changes you.

When you speak your story out loud, repeatedly, intentionally, you start to own it differently. You start to see patterns you hadn't noticed. You start to understand your own journey in new ways.

You become more confident talking about your message because you've practiced articulating it clearly.

You become more comfortable with your own voice because you've heard it saying meaningful things.

You become more aware of your own wisdom because you've had to explain it to someone else.

The book is just the beginning. The real transformation is in how speaking your truth changes your relationship with your own story and message.

YOUR BOOK SOUNDS LIKE YOU BECAUSE IT IS YOU

At the end of the day, the goal of transcription and editing isn't to turn your voice notes into something that sounds like a "real book." It's to turn your voice notes into a real book that sounds like you.

Because here's what I've learned after helping hundreds of people birth their books: the books that change lives aren't the ones that sound like they could have been written by anyone. They're the ones that sound like they could only have been written by one specific person—the person who lived the experience, learned the lessons, and cared enough to share what they discovered.

Your voice notes contain that book. The transcription and editing process is just about helping it emerge in its full power.

Roz was right: she had the story. But seeing it transcribed, organized, and polished helped her see that what she had was actually a book—one that would help other people navigate their own journeys with more wisdom and less struggle.

That's what transcription and transformation do: they help you see that what you've been carrying around in your voice and your experience is exactly what someone else needs to hear.

VOICE PROMPTS FOR CHAPTER 7

These prompts will help you think about the editing and polishing phase of your book.

Prompt 1: What is my biggest fear about turning this into a 'real' book? (6 minutes) Be honest about what scares you about the editing and publishing process. Naming these fears helps you address them constructively instead of letting them stop your progress.

Prompt 2: How do I want the finished product to feel? (8 minutes) Not just how you want it to look, but how you want readers to feel when they read it. Warm? Empowered? Understood? Challenged? This feeling should guide your editing decisions.

Prompt 3: What would I want someone to say about my book's voice and tone? (6 minutes) If someone described how your book "sounds" to them, what would you want them to say? This will help you communicate with editors about preserving what matters most about your authentic voice.

These recordings will help you approach the editing process with clarity about what you want to preserve and what you're willing to change.

CHAPTER 8

Publish Without Permission

*"I didn't want to just publish a book,
I wanted to steward my story well."*
— Roz

THE BIGGEST LIE in the publishing world is that you need someone else's permission to share your story.

You don't need a literary agent to validate that your book is worth reading. You don't need a traditional publisher to confirm that your message matters. You don't need anyone's approval to claim your space as an author.

What you need is clarity about your goals, understanding of your options, and the courage to move forward on your own terms.

MY PUBLISHING JOURNEY: LEARNING FROM MULTIPLE PATHS

Before we dive into your options, let me share something important: I'm speaking from experience across multiple publishing models.

I'm an 11-time published author and 2-time bestseller—once with Amazon and once with Barnes & Noble. I've worked with different publishing companies including James Morgan Press, The 1 And Only Publishing and Fit N Faith Press. I've self-published independently, and I've experienced the hybrid publishing model.

Currently, I work with The 1 And Only Publishing Company, a self-publishing and hybrid publishing company that helps authors maintain control while getting professional support. I'm sharing this upfront because I want you to understand both my experience and my current business relationship as we explore your publishing options.

What I've learned from this journey is that there's no single "right" way to publish. The right way is the one that aligns with your goals, timeline, budget, and comfort level. My job isn't to convince you to choose one path over another—it's to help you make an informed decision based on what matters most to you.

THE PERMISSION YOU'VE ALREADY BEEN GIVEN

Roz came to our conversation with questions about publishing that I hear from almost every author: "How long will it take to receive the first payment from Amazon after the book is published? What's the process for ensuring that third-party content is properly licensed? What about the timeline and costs?"

These are smart, practical questions. But underneath them was a deeper question: "Am I allowed to do this? Do I have permission to publish my story?"

Here's what I told her, and what I'm telling you: the moment you decided your story mattered enough to share, you gave yourself all the permission you need.

Your lived experience is your credential. Your wisdom earned through struggle and growth is your authority. Your desire to help others navigate what you've navigated is your mandate.

No one else can give you permission to tell your story because no one else has lived it.

UNDERSTANDING YOUR PUBLISHING OPTIONS

But permission to publish doesn't mean publishing without a plan. You need to understand your options so you can make informed decisions about how to get your book into the world.

Traditional Publishing means finding a literary agent who will pitch your book to publishing houses. If a publisher wants your book, they'll give you an advance against future royalties and handle the production, distribution, and (some) marketing.

- **The pros:** Potentially wide distribution, professional editing and design, some marketing support, the prestige of being "traditionally published."
- **The cons:** You give up control of your book, your timeline, and most of your profits. The process can take years. Most manuscripts are rejected. Even if you're accepted, the publisher owns your work and makes most of the decisions about how it's marketed and sold.

Self-Publishing means you maintain complete control of your book and keep all the profits, but you're responsible for all the costs and decisions around editing, design, production, distribution, and marketing.

- **The pros:** Complete creative and financial control, faster timeline, you keep all the royalties, your book stays in print as long as you want.
- **The cons:** Upfront costs, you're responsible for quality control, you handle all marketing, you need to learn about ISBN numbers and distribution channels.

Hybrid Publishing combines elements of both traditional and self-publishing. You invest in professional services (editing, design, marketing support) while retaining ownership of your book and keeping higher royalty percentages than traditional publishing.

- **The pros:** Professional quality with more control than traditional publishing, faster than traditional timeline, expert guidance through the process, support with marketing, you retain ownership and rights to your work.
- **The cons:** Upfront investment required, not all hybrid publishers are created equal (it's crucial to research and choose reputable companies), you're still actively involved in marketing your book.

I've had positive experiences with hybrid publishing because it gave me access to professional teams while letting me maintain control of my book and keep the majority of my profits. For many voice-first authors, this model provides the best balance of professional support and creative control.

CHOOSING THE RIGHT PATH FOR YOUR GOALS

Here's what I've discovered through my own publishing journey: both self-publishing and hybrid publishing can be excellent choices for voice-first authors. The key is understanding which approach serves your specific goals.

Self-publishing works well if:
- You want maximum control over every aspect of your book
- You have the time and inclination to manage the publishing process
- You want to keep the highest percentage of profits
- You already have professional contacts (editors, designers, etc.) or are willing to find them
- You're comfortable learning about ISBN numbers, distribution, and marketing

Hybrid publishing works well if:
- You want professional support throughout the process
- You prefer having an experienced team guide you through publishing
- You want access to professional services without having to coordinate multiple freelancers
- You value having someone to answer your questions and troubleshoot problems
- You're willing to invest upfront for comprehensive support

Both paths can result in professional-quality books that compete effectively in the marketplace. Both can lead to bestseller status—I've achieved it through different models.

The difference is in the experience and level of support you receive along the way.

ROYALTIES VS. REVENUE: UNDERSTANDING THE NUMBERS

One of the questions Roz asked was about payment timelines and processes. This touches on something crucial that many authors don't understand: the difference between royalties and revenue.

When you traditionally publish, you earn royalties—a percentage of the book's sale price. Typically 10-15% for hardcover books, less for paperbacks and ebooks. So if your book sells for $20, you might earn $2-3 per book. And you only start earning money after you've "earned out" your advance.

When you self-publish, you earn revenue—the difference between what the book sells for and what it costs to produce and distribute. On a $20 book sold through Amazon, you might earn $4-6 per book after printing costs and Amazon's cut.

That's still 2-3 times more money per book sold than traditional publishing.

Plus, you get paid monthly instead of waiting for annual royalty statements. And you don't have to earn out an advance before you see any money.

The math is still compelling: even with these margins, you need to sell fewer books as a self-published author to make the same amount of money as a traditionally published author.

ISBNS, DISTRIBUTION, AND MAKING IT OFFICIAL

Roz asked about the technical aspects of publishing, and these details matter because they affect how professional and widely available your book appears.

ISBN numbers are like social security numbers for books. They identify your specific book and designate you as the publisher. You can buy them directly from Bowker (in the US) or sometimes get them free from your publishing platform, though this means the platform is listed as your publisher.

Distribution channels determine where readers can buy your book. Amazon KDP gets you into Amazon (obviously) and makes your book available to other retailers. IngramSpark distributes to bookstores and libraries worldwide. Many authors use both for maximum reach.

Print-on-demand means books are printed when they're ordered, so you don't need to invest in inventory or worry about storage and shipping.

Ebook distribution through platforms like Draft2Digital can get your book into Apple Books, Barnes & Noble, Kobo, and other ebook retailers.

The technology exists to make your self-published book as professionally available as any traditionally published book. You don't need a publisher to access readers worldwide.

THE IMPORTANCE OF PROFESSIONAL HELP

Regardless of which publishing path you choose, here's something I cannot emphasize enough: invest in professional help.

Publishing a book is not a DIY project. Even if you choose to self-publish and maintain complete control, you still need:

- Professional editing to ensure your book is clear, compelling, and error-free
- Professional cover design because readers absolutely judge books by their covers
- Professional interior formatting so your book looks polished and reads smoothly
- Strategic marketing guidance to help readers discover your book

The difference between self-publishing and hybrid publishing isn't whether you get professional help—it's how you access and coordinate that help.

With self-publishing, you hire individual freelancers and manage the process yourself. With hybrid publishing, you work with a team that coordinates these services for you.

Both approaches can produce excellent results when you work with qualified professionals. The key is doing your research and choosing reputable people or companies to work with.

If you're considering hybrid publishing, look for companies that are transparent about their processes, let you retain ownership of your work, and have a track record of helping authors succeed. Companies like The 1 And Only Publishing Company focus on providing professional support while ensuring authors maintain control of their books and keep the majority of their profits.

QUALITY CONTROL: PROFESSIONAL WITHOUT COMPROMISE

"I didn't want to just publish a book," Roz told me. "I wanted to steward my story well."

This is the key to successful publishing, regardless of your chosen path: understanding that independence or professional support doesn't mean compromising on quality.

THE MARKETING REALITY

Here's something traditional publishers don't want you to know: even traditionally published authors have to do most of their own marketing.

Unless you're already famous or your publisher is investing heavily in your launch (which happens for very few books), you'll be responsible for:

- Building your platform and audience
- Speaking at events and on podcasts
- Managing your social media presence
- Connecting with bloggers and reviewers
- Organizing book signings and launch events

If you're going to do the marketing work anyway, why give away most of your profits to a publisher?

Self-publishing lets you keep control of your marketing message and timeline. You can launch when you're ready. You can target the exact audience you want to reach. You can adjust your strategy based on what's working.

YOUR PUBLISHING TIMELINE

One of Roz's concerns was timing—how long the publishing process takes and when she could expect to see results.

Here's the beautiful thing about self-publishing: you control the timeline.

From finished manuscript to published book can be as little as 2-4 weeks if you have your professional team in place.

Compare that to 12-24 months for traditional publishing, and 6-12 months for most hybrid publishers.

You can also control your launch strategy. Maybe you want to do a soft launch to test your marketing approach. Maybe you want to build buzz over several months before your official launch. Maybe you want to coordinate with a speaking engagement or media appearance.

When you own your publishing process, you make these decisions based on what serves your goals, not what serves someone else's publishing schedule.

THE COURAGE TO OWN YOUR STORY

Publishing without permission—whether through self-publishing or hybrid publishing—requires courage. Courage to trust that your story matters even if traditional gatekeepers haven't validated it. Courage to invest in yourself and your message. Courage to learn new skills and make decisions about things you've never had to think about before.

But here's what I've learned after my own publishing journey across multiple models: the courage to publish independently is the same courage that got you to speak your story in the first place.

You've already done the hardest part. You've found your voice, captured your truth, and shaped it into something that can help others. Publishing is just the bridge between your story and the people who need to hear it.

Roz was worried about stewarding her story well. What she discovered was that both self-publishing and hybrid publishing could give her control over that stewardship—she just needed to choose the path that felt right for her goals and comfort level.

Whether you choose to self-publish with a team of freelancers or work with a reputable hybrid publisher, you're still claiming ownership of your story and your right to share it with the world.

THE PERMISSION YOU GIVE OTHERS

When you publish without permission—when you claim your authority as an author and share your story on your own terms—you do something powerful beyond getting your book into the world.

You give other people permission to do the same.

Every voice-first book that gets published makes it easier for the next person to believe their story matters too. Every authentic voice that cuts through the noise of traditional publishing makes space for more authentic voices.

Your book isn't just your story shared. It's an invitation for others to share theirs.

VOICE PROMPTS FOR CHAPTER 8

These prompts will help you clarify your publishing goals and overcome any permission-seeking that might be holding you back.

Prompt 1: What myths did I believe about publishing? (7 minutes) Be honest about any false beliefs you've held about who gets to publish books, what makes someone "qualified" to be an author, or what you need before you can share your story.

Prompt 2: Why is it important to own my story AND my rights? (8 minutes) Think about why maintaining ownership of your book matters to you, whether you self-publish or work with a hybrid publisher. How do you want your story to be shared? What feels important about staying in control of that process while still getting professional support?

Prompt 3: What would it mean to me to hold my published book in my hands? (5 minutes) Get specific about what publication represents to you. How would it feel to know your story is available to help others? What would change in how you see yourself as an author?

Prompt 4: Which publishing path feels most aligned with my goals and comfort level? (7 minutes) Based on what you've learned about self-publishing and hybrid publishing, which approach appeals to you more? What factors are most important in your decision—control, support, timeline, budget, or something else?

These recordings will help you move from asking for permission to claiming your authority as the author of your own story.

CHAPTER 9

Build Your Audience Before You Launch

"My story started in a voice note and went viral as a reel. The book came after."
– Meme

THE BIGGEST MISTAKE most authors make isn't in writing their book or even in publishing it. It's in waiting until after their book is finished to start building relationships with the people who need to read it.

Your book launch shouldn't be the first time anyone hears about your story. It should be the culmination of conversations you've been having for months.

THE PRE-LAUNCH ADVANTAGE

During our publishing workshop, I shared statistics that surprise most authors: the average author spends $700 per month on marketing and 32 hours per month promoting their book. Yet 78% of authors say marketing is the hardest part of publishing.

Here's why: they're trying to build an audience for a book instead of building an audience for their message.

When you start marketing your message months before your book is published, several powerful things happen:

You discover what resonates most with your audience, which helps you refine your book's focus.

You build genuine relationships instead of just trying to sell something.

You create anticipation for your book among people who are already invested in your story.

You practice talking about your message, which makes you more confident and compelling when your book launches.

You get feedback that helps you improve your book before it's published.

YOUR VOICE NOTES AS CONTENT STRATEGY

Here's something beautiful about the voice-first method: your book creation process naturally generates your marketing content.

Those voice notes you recorded while developing your book? They're social media posts waiting to happen.

Those stories you captured about key moments in your journey? They're podcast interview material.

Those insights you spoke about what you learned? They're blog posts and newsletter content.

The prompts you answered about your transformation? They're the foundation of speaking topics and workshop content.

Brendamaris discovered this when she started sharing pieces of her story on social media. "My story started in a voice note and went viral as a reel," she told me. "The book came after."

She wasn't trying to market a book that didn't exist yet. She was sharing her authentic experience, and people connected with it. By the time her book was published, she already had an engaged audience who wanted to read the full story.

THE 90-DAY PRE-LAUNCH STRATEGY

Based on what I've learned from working with bestselling authors, here's the timeline that creates the most momentum for a book launch:

- **90 days before launch: Start sharing your message** Begin posting content related to your book's themes. Share insights, ask questions, tell pieces of your story. Focus on providing value, not selling anything.
- **60 days before launch: Announce your book** Let your audience know a book is coming. Share why you wrote it, who it's for, and what problem it solves. Start building anticipation.
- **30 days before launch: Open pre-orders** Make your book available for pre-order and give people compelling

reasons to order early—exclusive content, special pricing, or bonus materials.
- **Launch week: Celebrate with your community** By this point, you're not trying to convince strangers to buy your book. You're celebrating with people who are already excited about it.

BUILDING YOUR LAUNCH TEAM

Roz started our conversation about book launches with a small support team—her husband and four young women who believed in her message. I told her she needed to think bigger.

"You should aim for a launch team of 100 people," I said. "People who will share information about your book, leave reviews, and help spread the word."

This might sound overwhelming, but remember: you're not asking strangers to help you. You're inviting people who already know and trust you to be part of something meaningful.

Your launch team might include:

- Family and friends who've been following your journey
- Colleagues and professional connections
- People you've met through speaking or networking
- Online followers who engage with your content
- Anyone who's ever said "you should write a book"

The goal isn't to gather 100 people to spam their networks. It's to build a community of supporters who genuinely want your book to succeed because they believe in your message.

CONTENT THAT CONNECTS

The content you share while building your audience should do three things:

- **Provide value.** Share insights, tips, stories, or perspectives that help people, even if they never buy your book.
- **Build connection.** Let people get to know you as a person, not just as an author promoting a book.
- **Create anticipation.** Give glimpses of what's coming without giving everything away.

Your voice notes make this easy because they're already authentic, valuable, and personal. You're not creating marketing content from scratch—you're sharing pieces of the wisdom you've already captured.

LEVERAGING YOUR NETWORK

During our workshop, I emphasized something that many authors overlook: you already have a network. You don't need to build an audience from zero.

Think about all the people who already know you:

- Coworkers and former colleagues
- Friends and family members
- People from your church, gym, or community organizations
- Professional connections on LinkedIn
- Social media followers, even if it's a small number
- Anyone who's ever asked for your advice on the topic of your book

These people are your starting point. They're the foundation of your launch team.

But here's the key: don't just ask them to buy your book when it's published. Invite them into your journey while you're creating it.

Share updates about your progress. Ask for their input on cover designs or book titles. Let them know how the writing process is going. When they feel invested in your journey, they'll be excited to celebrate your success.

THE POWER OF PRE-ORDERS

Pre-orders are powerful for several reasons:

- **They boost your launch week sales,** which can help you hit bestseller lists.
- **They provide social proof** that people want your book.
- **They create commitment** from your audience—when someone pre-orders, they're more likely to actually read and review your book.
- **They give you data** about how much interest exists for your book.

But pre-orders only work if you've built anticipation first. You can't just announce a book and expect people to order it. You need to spend time sharing your message and building relationships.

SPEAKING YOUR WAY TO AN AUDIENCE

One of the most effective ways to build an audience for your book is to start speaking about your message.

This might mean:

- Appearing on podcasts related to your topic
- Speaking at local organizations or events
- Hosting workshops or webinars
- Creating your own podcast or video series
- Offering to speak at conferences in your field

The beautiful thing about voice-first authors is that you're already comfortable talking about your message. You've practiced articulating your insights through your voice notes. You know how to tell your story in a compelling way.

Speaking engagements serve multiple purposes:
- They help you refine your message
- They connect you with potential readers
- They establish you as an expert in your field
- They provide content for social media and marketing
- They can lead to book sales and ongoing relationships

MEASURING WHAT MATTERS

As you build your audience, focus on quality over quantity. It's better to have 100 people who are genuinely interested in your message than 1,000 people who don't engage with your content.

Track metrics that actually matter:

- How many people are engaging with your content (comments, shares, saves)
- How many people are joining your email list
- How many people are asking questions about your book
- How many pre-orders you're getting
- How many speaking opportunities you're booking

Don't get caught up in vanity metrics like total follower

count. Focus on building genuine relationships with people who care about your message.

THE LONG GAME

Building an audience isn't just about launching one book. It's about creating a platform for sharing your message over time.

Your first book might lead to speaking opportunities, which lead to coaching clients, which lead to your second book. Or it might open doors to media appearances, which expand your audience, which creates opportunities for partnerships and collaborations.

When you build an audience for your message rather than just for a single book, you're investing in a long-term platform for impact.

Brendamaris understood this. Her viral reel wasn't just marketing for her book—it was the beginning of a larger conversation about her message. The book became one way she shared that message, but not the only way.

STARTING WHERE YOU ARE

You don't need a massive platform to start building an audience for your book. You just need to start where you are, with the people you already know, sharing the message you already have.

Your voice notes contain the content. Your network contains the starting audience. Your story contains the value people are looking for.

The bridge between your message and the people who need to hear it isn't built overnight. But it is built one authentic conversation at a time.

VOICE PROMPTS FOR CHAPTER 9

These prompts will help you think strategically about building an audience for your book.

Prompt 1: What's one way I've shown up powerfully for my audience already? (6 minutes) Think about times when you've helped people, shared wisdom, or made a difference in someone's life. How can you do more of this as you build toward your book launch?

Prompt 2: What part of my voice resonates most with others? (8 minutes) Based on feedback you've received or reactions to your story, what aspects of your message seem to connect most strongly with people? How can you emphasize these elements in your pre-launch content?

Prompt 3: Who are 20 people I could ask to be part of my launch team? (6 minutes) Start with people who already know and support you. Who would be genuinely excited to help you share your book? Don't edit yourself—just brainstorm names of potential supporters.

These recordings will help you shift from thinking about marketing as promotion to thinking about it as relationship-building and community creation.

CHAPTER 10

Monetize the Message

*"The book wasn't the end. It was the
engine for everything else."*
— Terry

YOUR BOOK is not your business model. Your book is your business card.

This might be the most important thing you learn about publishing: books rarely make authors rich through book sales alone. But they can transform your entire professional life by positioning you as an expert, opening doors to new opportunities, and creating a platform for sharing your message in multiple ways.

The goal isn't to make money from your book. The goal is to make money because of your book.

BEYOND BOOK SALES: THE REAL ROI

During our work together, Terry Williams discovered something that shifted his entire perspective on publishing. His book wasn't going to replace his income through royalties. But it was going to amplify his existing business in ways he hadn't anticipated.

"The book wasn't the end," he told me. "It was the engine for everything else."

I knew exactly what he meant because I had experienced this first hand after my first book:

My coaching rates increased because I could position myself as a published author and expert.

Speaking opportunities multiplied because event organizers wanted someone who had written the book on my topic.

My webinars filled faster because potential clients could read my book first and arrive already convinced of my expertise.

Media opportunities opened up because journalists and podcasters prefer interviewing published authors.

Strategic partnerships emerged because other professionals saw me as a credible collaborator.

The book sales were nice, but the business impact was transformational.

YOUR BOOK AS PLATFORM BUILDER

Think of your book as the foundation of a larger platform for sharing your message. That platform might include:

- **Speaking and training.** Your book establishes your expertise and gives event organizers confidence in booking

you. You can command higher fees as a published author, and your book can be sold at events for additional revenue.
- **Coaching and consulting.** Your book serves as a 200-page sales letter for your services. Potential clients can get to know your approach, philosophy, and personality before they ever speak with you.
- **Online courses and programs.** Your book content can be expanded into comprehensive training programs. People who love your book will want to go deeper with your teaching.
- **Workshops and retreats.** Your book can be the curriculum for in-person or virtual events where you teach your methodology in an interactive format.
- **Licensing and certification.** If you've developed a unique framework or system, you might eventually license it to other professionals or create certification programs.

THE ECOSYSTEM APPROACH

The most successful voice-first authors think in terms of creating an ecosystem around their message, not just publishing a single book.

Here's how this might look:

The book introduces your message and builds your audience.

- **A podcast or video series** allows you to explore topics from your book in more depth and interview other experts.

- **A newsletter or blog** keeps you connected with readers and provides ongoing value.
- **Speaking engagements** let you share your message with new audiences and generate income.
- **Coaching or consulting** provides personalized help for people who want to apply your principles to their specific situations.
- **Courses or programs** offer structured ways for people to learn your methodology.
- **Community or membership** creates ongoing connection among people interested in your message.

Each element supports and amplifies the others. Your book drives people to your speaking events. Your speaking events drive people to your coaching services. Your coaching clients become testimonials for your book and courses.

PRICING YOUR EXPERTISE

One of the most significant changes that happens after you publish a book is how you price your time and expertise.

As a published author, you can typically:

- **Increase your consulting or coaching rates** by 50-100% or more.
- **Command higher speaking fees** because you're seen as a credible expert.
- **Charge premium prices for courses and programs** because you have proven content.
- **Attract higher-quality clients** who are willing to invest in working with an expert.

This isn't about inflating your prices artificially. It's about being appropriately compensated for the value you provide. Your book serves as proof of your expertise and differentiates you from others in your field.

THE CONTENT MULTIPLICATION EFFECT

Your voice notes don't just become a book—they become content for multiple platforms and revenue streams.

- **Podcast episodes:** Each chapter of your book could become a podcast episode, with additional thoughts and examples.
- **Workshop modules:** Your book's framework can be taught in live workshops or online courses.
- **Social media content:** Key insights from your book provide months of social media posts.
- **Speaking topics:** Different aspects of your book become different keynote presentations.
- **Blog posts and articles:** You can write for publications in your field, positioning yourself as the expert who wrote the book on the topic.
- **Video content:** Your stories and insights can be shared through video for different audiences and platforms.

The content creation work you do for your book pays dividends across multiple channels for years to come.

BUILDING STRATEGIC PARTNERSHIPS

Your book opens doors to collaborations and partnerships that wouldn't have been possible before.

Other authors might invite you to contribute to their books or projects.

Business leaders might want to partner with you on programs or initiatives.

Media outlets might seek your expert commentary on relevant topics.

Organizations might hire you to create custom training based on your book's principles.

These partnerships often become more lucrative than book sales themselves, while also expanding your reach and credibility.

THE SPEAKING CIRCUIT

For many voice-first authors, speaking becomes the primary way they monetize their message.

Your book serves as:

- Credibility for booking agents and event organizers
- Content for multiple different presentations
- Product to sell at the back of the room
- Follow-up tool for connecting with audience members after events

Speaking fees can range from a few hundred dollars for local events to tens of thousands for major conferences. And unlike book royalties, speaking fees are immediate income.

CREATING PASSIVE INCOME STREAMS

While you're building your platform through speaking and coaching, you can also create income streams that don't require your direct time:

- **Online courses** that teach your book's methodology can generate revenue while you sleep.
- **Digital products** like worksheets, assessments, or templates related to your book can provide ongoing income.
- **Affiliate partnerships** with tools or resources you recommend can create additional revenue.
- **Licensing deals** where others pay to use your content or methodology can provide recurring income.

The key is to create these streams after you've established your expertise and built an audience, not before.

THE LONG-TERM VISION

Terry understood something crucial: building a business around your message is a long-term game. Your first book might generate modest direct income, but it's the foundation for everything that comes after.

Many successful authors write multiple books, each one building on the platform created by the previous ones. Each book expands their audience, deepens their expertise, and opens new opportunities.

Some authors eventually build companies around their message, hiring teams to help them serve more people. Others prefer to stay solo but charge premium rates for their time. Both approaches can be financially successful.

STARTING THE MONETIZATION CONVERSATION EARLY

Here's something most authors don't realize: you should start thinking about monetizing your message before your book is even published.

As you're building your audience and sharing your content, pay attention to:

- What questions people ask most frequently
- What problems they want help solving
- How they prefer to consume your content
- What they're willing to pay for

This market research will inform how you structure your post-publication offerings.

You might discover that people want group coaching, or one-on-one consulting, or online courses, or live workshops. Understanding this before you publish helps you plan your business development strategy.

YOUR MESSAGE AS YOUR MISSION

The most successful authors who monetize their message do so because they're genuinely passionate about helping people, not just making money.

When Terry talks about his coaching work, you can hear the genuine satisfaction he gets from helping people organize their potential and take action. The income is important, but the impact is what drives him.

When you're building a business around your book, remember that your message is your mission. The money follows when you focus on truly serving the people who need what you have to offer.

Your voice notes captured something valuable—wisdom that can help others navigate challenges you've already overcome. Monetizing that wisdom isn't just about building a business; it's about creating sustainable ways to share your message with more people over time.

VOICE PROMPTS FOR CHAPTER 10

These prompts will help you envision the business opportunities that could grow from your book.

- **Prompt 1: How could my story help someone else grow?** (8 minutes) Think beyond just reading your book. How could you personally help someone apply your insights to their situation? What would coaching or consulting from you look like?
- **Prompt 2: What product, service, or talk naturally flows from this message?** (7 minutes) Based on your book's content, what other ways could you share this message? What would people want to learn more about? What problems could you help solve?
- **Prompt 3: What would my ideal business look like in 3 years?** (10 minutes) If your book became the foundation for a larger platform, what would you want that to look like? How would you want to spend your time? What kind of impact would you want to have?

These recordings will help you start thinking strategically about the long-term potential of your voice-first book and message.

CONCLUSION

Say It Again

*"You didn't just help me write a book.
You helped me believe again."*
– Kristi

WE'VE COVERED a lot of ground together in these pages. You've learned about giving yourself permission to speak your story before you write it. You've discovered how to work with your natural rhythms and design sustainable creative habits. You've explored how to use prompts as GPS for your inner landscape and how to speak in color instead of chaos.

You've seen how voice notes transform into structure, how authentic transcription preserves your unique voice, and how to choose the publishing path that honors your goals. You've learned to build an audience for your message, not just your book, and discovered how your story can become the foundation for a larger platform of impact.

But most importantly, you've learned this: you don't need to write to be a writer. You just need to speak your truth and trust that your voice—exactly as it is—contains everything your book needs to be.

THE STORIES THAT STARTED IT ALL

Think back to the women whose voices you've heard throughout this book:

Brittney, who discovered that fifteen minutes of morning voice notes could birth a book that changed her life and the lives of her readers.

Kristi, who learned to stop performing on the page and start speaking authentically about her journey from corporate burnout to purpose-driven life.

Tracy, who found the language for her spiritual transformation when she realized they had "tasted independence when he offered intimacy."

Sia, who understood that her specific, emotionally painful story was actually a universal human story that could heal others.

Terry, who discovered that his life had chapters—he just needed to name them and organize them into a framework that could help others.

Lady Roz, who realized she had the story all along and just needed help making it into a book that could serve her community.

Each of these women had the same three things you have right now:

- A story that mattered
- A voice that could tell it

- A desire to help others

That's all you need. Everything else—the technology, the structure, the publishing path, the marketing strategy—those are just tools to help your story reach the people who need to hear it.

WHAT'S POSSIBLE WHEN YOU SAY IT

When you give yourself permission to speak your story into existence, something magical happens. It's not just that you create a book (though you do). It's not just that you help other people (though you will).

It's that you change your relationship with your own voice, your own wisdom, your own authority.

You stop waiting for permission to claim your expertise.

You stop apologizing for taking up space.

You stop believing that your story isn't dramatic enough, polished enough, or important enough to matter.

You start owning what you know, trusting what you've learned, and sharing what you've discovered.

The ripple effects are profound. Your book becomes a business card for opportunities you didn't even know you wanted. Your message becomes a platform for impact you couldn't have imagined. Your voice becomes a tool for transformation—not just for your readers, but for yourself.

THE VOICE THAT'S BEEN WAITING

Your book is already inside you. It's been waiting in every conversation where you've helped someone see their situation differently. It's been forming in every moment when you've shared hard-won wisdom with a friend. It's been growing stronger every time you've said, "You know what I learned when I went through something similar?"

That voice—the one that shows up when you're explaining something you're passionate about, when you're comforting someone who's struggling, when you're celebrating someone's breakthrough—that's your book voice.

It doesn't need to be polished. It needs to be real.

It doesn't need to sound like other authors. It needs to sound like you.

It doesn't need permission from publishers or agents or anyone else. It needs permission from you.

YOUR STORY MATTERS

I'll say it one more time, because it bears repeating: your story matters.

Not because it's more dramatic than someone else's. Not because you've overcome more obstacles or achieved more success. Not because you have advanced degrees or impressive credentials.

Your story matters because it's yours. Because you've lived it, learned from it, and survived it. Because somewhere out there is someone who needs to hear exactly what you have to say, in exactly the way you would say it.

They're not waiting for the perfect book. They're waiting for the real book. The one that sounds like a conversation with someone who understands what they're going through.

They're waiting for your book.

THE INVITATION

So here's my invitation to you: stop waiting for someday. Stop believing you need more time, better circumstances, different qualifications, or someone else's permission.

Start where you are. Use what you have. Say what you know.

Push record on your phone and answer this question: "What do I wish I could tell the world?"

Then answer this one: "What do I wish someone had told me five years ago?"

And this one: "What wisdom have I earned through just living my life?"

Those answers? That's your book talking.

Listen to what it has to say. Trust what it knows. Give it the voice it deserves.

READY TO DISCOVER HOW READY YOU ARE?

If you're feeling that stirring in your spirit—that sense that your story is ready to be born—I want to help you take the next step.

I've created a Story Readiness Quiz that will help you discover exactly where you are in your journey from idea to published book. In just a few minutes, you'll get clarity on:

- How ready your story is to be shared
- What your next best step should be
- Which aspects of the voice-first method will serve you most
- How to move forward with confidence

You can take the quiz right now at https://jorioneale.com/**your-story-matters**

Because here's what I've learned after helping hundreds of women birth their books: the perfect time to start is now. Not when you have more time. Not when you feel more ready. Not when circumstances are ideal.

Now. With your real life, your authentic voice, and your important story.

Your book is waiting for you to say it into existence.

The world is waiting to hear what you have to say.

And I'm here to help you talk your book from your heart to the hands of the people who need it most.

It's time to say it. Shape it. Share it.

It's time to talk your book.

Jori O'Neale

International Best Selling Author, Writer, Speaker, Podcast Host

Signature Podcast

Jori O'Neale is a highly sought-after speaker and trainer with 18+ years as an educator. She's the CEO and co-founder of IYH INNERTAINMENT LLC, a faith-based entertainment company building community through creative works. A 10-time published, 2-time best-selling author and publishing authority partner, Jori equips aspiring authors to turn life experiences into transformational books—without the overwhelm. After leaving a stable six-figure career to follow her God-given purpose, she now inspires others to stop settling and boldly share their stories.

"EMPOWERING PURPOSE-DRIVEN VOICES TO BE HEARD!"

Signature Topics

✓ The Power of Your Story
✓ Unleash Your God Given Gifts
✓ History Determines Herstory

Signature Workshops

✓ Your Story Matters
✓ Uncover Your God Given Gifts
✓ The Productive Christian: How to Go from Striving to Thriving

Companies Worked With

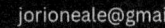 jorioneale@gmail.com   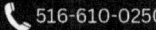 516-610-2450    @jorioneale

contact me to learn more: https://jorioneale.com

www.ingramcontent.com/pod-product-compliance
Lightning Source LLC
Chambersburg PA
CBHW070809230426
43665CB00017B/2543